ROOTING FOR PLANTS

The Unstoppable Charles S. Parker, Black Botanist and Collector

Janice N. Harrington   Illustrated by Theodore Taylor III

CALKINS CREEK
AN IMPRINT OF ASTRA BOOKS FOR YOUNG READERS
New York

PROLOGUE: BEGIN WITH A PLANT

Its petals looked like tiny slippers, and green pods dangled from its stems. Other people might have huffed *Weed!* and gone on their way. But not Charles. He scraped the grasslike plant from the soil and hurried back to his college laboratory. Charles Stewart Parker loved plants, and he loved learning about them.

He wanted to know *where*, *when*, *why*, and *how* they grew. He wanted people to go into the wondrous green world and maybe, with his help, learn to love plants, too.

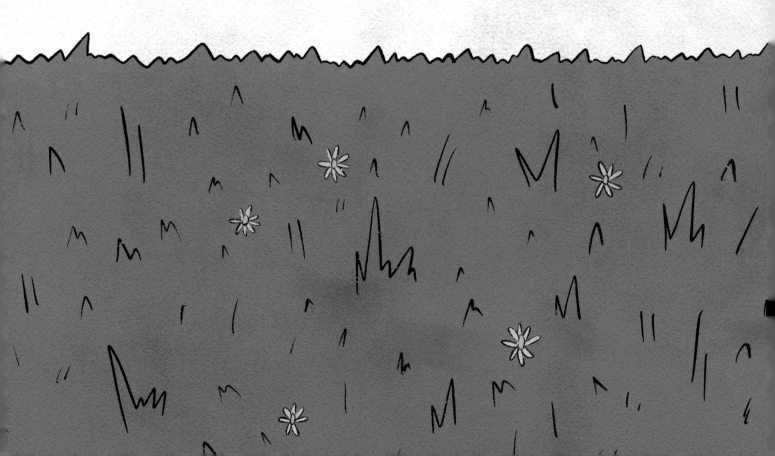

Charles grew up surrounded by green: green forests where conifers tickled the sky, green banks washed by the rolling Spokane River, and the lush everywhere-green of Spokane, Washington. And like the winds over the green grasses of the Palouse, Charles S. Parker moved fast.

On the racetrack he drove his legs over the finish line,
and in the classroom his quick mind raced through
homework and good books. Folks called him "brainy boy."
    The brainy Charles came from a family of achievers: a
barber-inventor, a businesswoman, a debater, two champion
athletes, and a quick-fingered pianist. The talented Parkers
believed in working hard and helping others.

Charles did both.
At twenty-six, Charles and his best friend started a newspaper they called the *Citizen*. He wrote about life in Spokane and new jobs for Black workers.

Charles raced around the city and its surrounding farmlands searching for news. To Charles, the Spokane countryside looked like a big, green garden, a garden that planted a dream: Charles wanted to own a farm.

But in 1917, terrible news swept his dream aside. The United States was going to war!

US IS AT WAR!

In a shady grove, Lieutenant Charles S. Parker typed a letter home about the Black soldiers of the 366th Infantry who sailed to France to help fight the German army.

Life wasn't easy for Black soldiers. When his men were commanded to eat later than white soldiers, Charles took action and persuaded his commanding officers to change the unfair orders. Some army officers even believed that a Black lieutenant couldn't lead men in battle. Charles was determined to prove them wrong.

Whishhh-boom! Shells burst, bullets buzzed, and poisonous gases choked the air. Charles scouted for enemy soldiers. Leading his men, he slogged through the mud and fought. His heart ached from seeing so many men die, but it swelled with pride for the brave Black soldiers.

Charles would never forget those grim battlefields.
He saw forests where green trees stood broken and
torched. He saw shell-blasted farms where nothing green
could grow. He saw gray mud, gray smoke, and gray thorny
wire. But inside, Charles still felt his bright dream.

After the Great War, Charles couldn't afford a farm. So he grew his dream another way. He taught *other* people how to farm, raise gardens, and plant orchards. He called himself a "consulting horticulturalist." But Charles's dream kept growing. He wanted to learn about all kinds of plants— not just plants that grew on farms.

At the State College of Washington, he studied botany, the science of plants. Armed with his field press, a botanical pick, and the new ideas his teachers taught him, Charles marched into the wild everywhere-green to botanize—to study plants in the outdoors.

Wanting to discover the plants that grew in the
Pacific Northwest and to learn how each fit into the world
of plants, Charles struggled up jagged peaks, trudged over
icy glaciers, trekked through forests, and waded into
stinky, slimy, ghost-colored salt lakes.

But once he found a plant, Charles also found a problem—how to preserve the plant so other scientists could study it, too.

ASPLENIUM TRICHOMANES
C.S. PARKER

Charles removed a dried fern from his field press. He taped its fronds to heavy paper and typed a label that explained where and when the fern grew. He wrote the fern's scientific name, *Asplenium trichomanes*, and the name of its collector: C. S. Parker. Charles made specimen mounts to add to the school's herbarium, its library of dried plants. Specimen mounts helped plant taxonomists, like Charles, identify plants and examine plant structure.

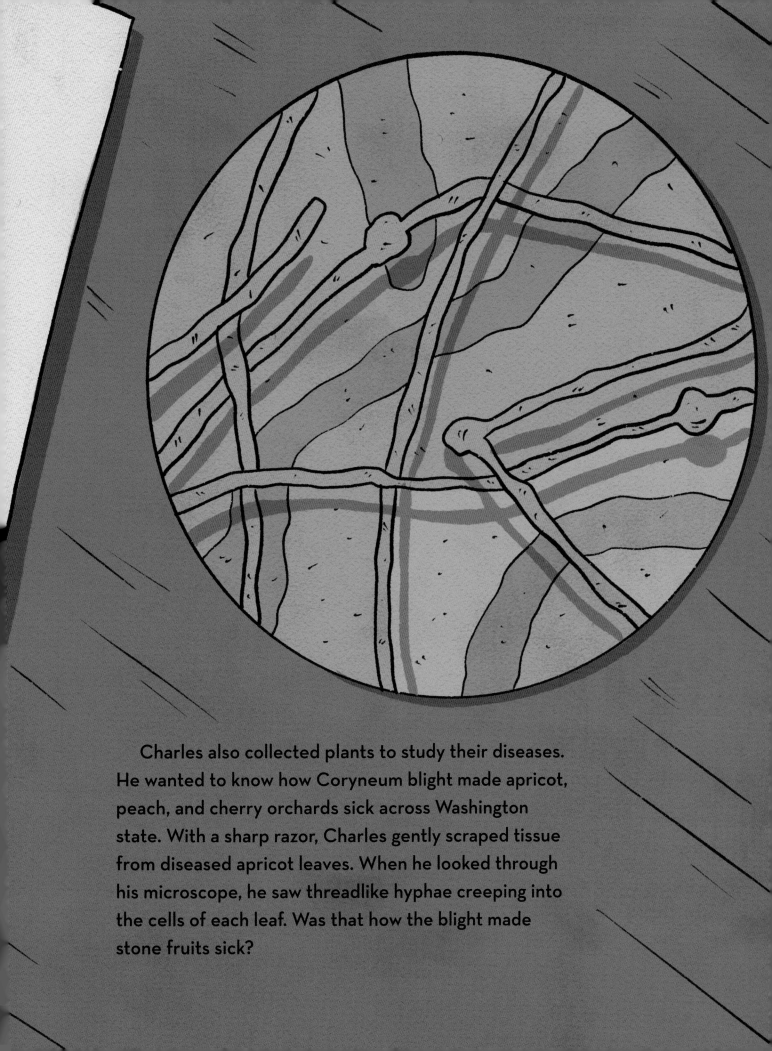

Charles also collected plants to study their diseases. He wanted to know how Coryneum blight made apricot, peach, and cherry orchards sick across Washington state. With a sharp razor, Charles gently scraped tissue from diseased apricot leaves. When he looked through his microscope, he saw threadlike hyphae creeping into the cells of each leaf. Was that how the blight made stone fruits sick?

News of his investigations reached Howard University, a school for Black students in Washington, DC. The president of Howard offered a job to the "marvelous man in botany."

In a cramped Howard laboratory, Charles urged his students to look and look again at the plants around them. Where did they grow? How were they similar to or different from other plants?

CORN CHAMOMILE

GOLDEN ASTERS

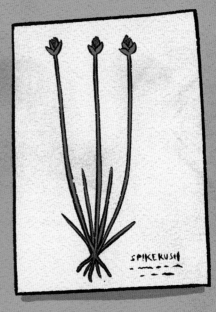

SPIKERUSH

CINNAMON FERN

SKUNK CABBAGE

MOUSE-EAR CHICKWEED

Charles answered these questions, too.
In woods, along bluffs, and beside the banks of the
Potomac River, Charles filled his field press with Maryland
plants: corn chamomile, golden asters, spikerush, cinnamon
fern, skunk cabbage, mouse-ear chickweed.

Charles had botanized in the West and the East, but now he wondered: What plants grew in the South?

Charles drove to South Carolina, Georgia, and Florida. He pulled orchids from mosquitoey ditches, dug giant yuccas from windswept dunes, tugged up prickly pears, plucked seeds from withered pods, and scooped up weeds that waves and wind carried from the West Indies. His car bulged from hood to trunk with cycads (ancient plants that grew when the dinosaurs lived), cacti, and hundreds of other plants.

The enthusiastic professor's whirlwind expedition made front-page news!

Charles loved learning about plants so much that he went back to school during the summer months to discover even more.

At the State College of Pennsylvania, the forty-eight-year-old Charles took classes with the mushroom-loving professor Lee Oras Overholts, who invited Charles on a bold botanical adventure.

In a pontoon plane, Charles roller coasted into the wilds of northern Canada. With eleven other scientists from Russia, Canada, and the United States, he studied how the climate affected the growth of mushrooms and other fungi.

Charles took notes and photographs. He gathered fungi and dug, dug, dug with his botanical pick. After the twenty-six-day expedition, the unstoppable plant hunter brought back two thousand new specimens for the Howard University Herbarium.

Driven by his new interest in mushrooms, molds, mildews, and other fungi, Charles saw that a mushroom called the *Hypholoma* needed more study. Charles photographed its mycelia, stipe, cap, and gills.

He measured the mushroom's spores and drew pictures to show its bowling-pin shape. He used his senses: taste, smell, sight, touch. He asked how each *Hypholoma* specimen was like or different from others and compared them under a microscope. In the outdoors, he gathered specimen after specimen until, at last, he was ready to tell a story.

Click-click! Charles typed. *Click-click!* Sometimes his words were Latin: *Hypholoma oblongisporum.* Sometimes his words were poetry: *floccose, fibrillose, filiform.* Sometimes they painted word pictures of each *Hypholoma.* Charles wrote the first study of a mushroom species by a Black American mycologist (a scientist who studies mushrooms). He was the first botanist to write a clear, organized description of the *Hypholoma!*

Charles introduced several new *Hypholoma* species to the botanical world, including *H. cinereum* C. S. Parker, *H. simile* C. S. Parker, and five other species. Each species name ended with "Parker" for the scientist who discovered it.

At Howard, Charles taught even more classes, harder classes, classes about plants and fungi and plant diseases. His students scraped tissue from green leaves and thin slices of roots to make microscope slides. They bent over their notebooks drawing mushroom caps or the petals of a wildflower. They taped dried stems to heavy sheets to make specimen mounts. They marched into the outdoors to botanize. They examined plants infected with hideous smuts and blights and rusts.

They asked questions—just like their teacher.
What helped chicory grow strong roots? How did
air pollution change the growth of fungi? How much
time does a mayapple need to bear fruit?

Charles said that his students nearly "worked me off my feet." But he didn't stop or slow down, because he knew that, sadly, the United States had only a few Black scientists. Worst of all, he knew that too many Black children grew up believing they could never be scientists, and too many young women believed that science was only for men.

In his classrooms, the veteran soldier fought to change those beliefs.

The plant collector who drew people out into the wondrous green world inspired hundreds of Black students, many of them young women, to blossom into pioneering scientists, teachers, and leaders. They never forgot "the most wonderful teacher they ever had."

GLOSSARY

blight: A plant disease.

botanical pick: A T-shaped tool for digging plants out of the ground.

botanize: Going into the outdoors to collect or study plants.

botany: The study of plants.

cap: The fleshy top of a mushroom.

fibrillose: Having a surface covered with small threads or fibers.

field press: A wooden frame used to dry plants flat for display, preservation, and scientific study.

filiform: Threadlike or thin. A mushroom's spores might look filiform under a microscope.

floccose: Having tufts of soft, woolly hairs or feeling woolly to the touch.

fungal spore: A one-celled body that fungi use to reproduce or make new fungi. Mushrooms grow from spores.

fungi: One of the six major groups (kingdoms) of biology. Mushrooms, toadstools, yeasts, rusts, smuts, mildews, and molds are examples of fungi.

gills: The thin papery ribs under a mushroom's cap.

grafting: Joining the tissues of two plants together to grow a new plant.

herbarium: A collection of dried plants.

horticulturist: A person who studies and grows gardens, orchards, or flowering plants.

hyphae: Long branching fibers on the mycelia of a fungus.

Hypholoma: A type of mushroom that grows on dead wood. One well-known hypholoma is called *sulphur tuft*.

laboratory: A room where scientists conduct studies, often using special equipment to test their ideas and explore scientific questions.

mycelium: The rootlike hairs that grow from the base of a mushroom. Some fungi only live as mycelia and never produce a mushroom.

mycologist: A scientist who studies, collects, and preserves fungi.

naturalist: A person who studies plants, animals, or other organisms.

organism: Any living thing.

plant collector: A person who collects plants for preservation, scientific study, or to add to gardens, greenhouse collections, or herbaria.

plant pathologist: A scientist who studies plant diseases.

plant physiologist: A scientist who studies plant functions, processes, or behavior.

rust: A fungus that looks like rusty metal. Rust attacks plants and causes plant disease.

smut: A fungus that attacks grains such as wheat or corn.

species: The basic unit of classification in biology, a group of related organisms that can mate and produce offspring.

specimen: A single example of a plant, animal, or object studied or displayed for science.

stipe: A mushroom's stalk or stem.

taxonomist: A scientist who identifies, sorts, and names organisms.

> "My field notebook shows that I have collected 947 species."

MORE ABOUT CHARLES STEWART PARKER

The Parkers moved to Spokane in the early 1880s. They were one of Spokane's pioneer families. John B. Parker owned a barbershop and invented a shaving tool called a razor castor, while Ordella Parker provided haircare for wealthy women. Unlike many Black children, Charles and his brothers and sister grew up well-to-do.

At seventeen, Charles attended King Theological Hall, a school in Washington, DC, where young Black men studied to become Episcopal ministers. There he also met and married a young school teacher, Annice M. Lewis.

Returning to Spokane, Charles grew into an active leader in the Black community. Voters elected the staunch Republican to the county auditor's office. With a wealthy friend, Charles started the *Citizen*, a newspaper for Spokane's Black community. A pioneering journalist and editor, Charles also ran the X-Ray Printing Company and invested in one of Washington's largest Black-owned businesses, an apple orchard that hired over one hundred Black workers. Charles served as the orchard's treasurer.

In 1917, when the United States entered World War I, the army was segregated: Black and white soldiers were not allowed to fight together. Despite this challenge, Charles became an officer with the 366th Infantry regiment.

Soon after the war, Charles taught horticulture at Booker T. Washington's Tuskegee Institute. Enrolling at the State College of Washington, he studied with Dr. Harold St. John. For his landmark book on the plants of Idaho and Southeast Washington, Dr. St. John used plant specimens that Charles and another student collected. He also named two plants in honor of his student and colleague: a Sierra pea (*Lathyrus nevadensis* var. *parkeri*) and a wild Nootka rose (*Rosa spaldingii* var. *parkeri*).

Charles held several jobs after graduating from the state college, but eventually he returned to Washington, DC, to teach at Paul Laurence Dunbar High School, America's first public Black high school. He then joined the faculty of Howard University, where he taught botany and curated the Howard University Herbarium. In 1928, Charles enrolled at the State College of Pennsylvania to earn a doctoral degree and to complete *A Taxonomic Study of the Genus* Hypholoma *in North America*. It would have surprised many Americans at the time (and even today) to learn that there were plants and fungi discovered by or named for a Black American scientist.

Returning to Howard, Charles continued to lead the Botany Department. He also launched Howard's master's program in botany.

Charles's work—as a botanist, naturalist, plant pathologist, herbarium curator, taxonomist, mycologist, and plant collector—stands out because he worked at a time when so few Black Americans were scientists. Until the civil rights gains of the 1960s, Black American scientists were often refused work, barred from scientific organizations, or frustrated to see their research ignored, slighted, or attributed to others. Charles served as a heroic soldier during World War I, and he also served as a heroic teacher who helped lay the groundwork for more Black Americans to become scientists.

Other scientists used Charles's botanical photographs and plant specimens in their research and writing. Botanists still study the plant and fungal specimens that he collected, and today his specimen mounts are found in herbaria throughout the United States and as far away as Brazil, including such leading herbaria as the Missouri Botanical Garden Herbarium, Chicago's Field Museum, the United States National Fungus Collection, the New York Botanical Garden Steere Herbarium, and the Howard University Herbarium, which faculty and students fondly call the Charles S. Parker Herbarium in honor of the pioneering botanist.

> "The pupil's mind is attracted to familiar parts of the plant
> and led into the unfamiliar."

TIMELINE

1882 Charles Stewart Parker born to John B. Parker and Ordella Parker, March 31 in Corinne, UT. The Parkers move to Spokane, WA, in the early 1880s. By 1894, he has three younger brothers and a younger sister: Byron, Harry, Douglas, and Candace.

1895–1898 Attends Spokane Central High School.

1899 Attends King Theological Hall in Washington, DC, where Black students studied to become Episcopal ministers.

1901 Marries Annice M. Lewis.

1902–1905 Attends Trinity College (according to a newspaper source, this college was in Oakland, CA). Writes in a 1904 newspaper article that he is studying for the ministry.

1908–1910 Runs the X-Ray Printing Company.

1908–1913 Starts the *Citizen*, a newspaper for Spokane's Black families, with his friend Charles S. Barrow. Works as an editor and a reporter for the paper, which grows to seven hundred subscribers.

1917–1919 Joins the army. One of four Black soldiers from Spokane who fought in World War I. Becomes one of the few Black officers among the American troops in World War I and serves in France in the 366th Infantry.

1919–1920   Teaches horticulture at Tuskegee Institute in Alabama.

1920–1923   Enrolls at the State College of Washington, where he earns bachelor and master of science degrees.

1923–1924   Works as a plant pathologist with the U.S. Bureau of Plant Industry in North Carolina. Teaches at North Carolina State College.

1925   Begins teaching at Paul Laurence Dunbar High School, Washington, DC. Begins teaching botany at Howard University, Washington, DC.

1928   Enrolls at State College of Pennsylvania. Begins study of the *Hypholoma*.

1930   Returns to Howard University as professor of botany.

1932   Earns a PhD in plant pathology from State College of Pennsylvania.

1937   Serves as head of the Department of Botany at Howard University from 1937-1947, and head of the Department of Zoology from 1939-1944.

1947   Retires from Howard University.

1950   Dies January 10 in Spokane, WA. Buried at Arlington National Cemetery in Arlington, VA.

Left top: Plants fascinated him.
Left middle: At Howard University
Left bottom: His specimen mount

OTHER BLACK BOTANISTS AND MYCOLOGISTS TO KNOW

George Washington Carver (1864–1943). Carver often comes to mind when people think of a Black botanist. Carver was a prominent agronomist, meaning that he studied crops and farming. He gained international fame for the new products he made from peanuts, sweet potatoes, and soybeans. But few people know that Carver, like Charles S. Parker, was also a pioneering mycologist. He worked with the mycologist Franklin Sumner Earle to compile a list of Alabama fungi. Today, the renowned New York Botanical Garden holds fungi collected by both Carver and Parker.

O'Neil Ray Collins (1931–1989). Like Charles S. Parker, Collins studied fungi. He discovered that slime mold, which begins as an amoeba-like cell, could reproduce alone or by mating with a partner. Collins chaired the Department of Botany at the University of California, Berkeley. He published more than seventy scientific papers, and he stands, like Parker, as one of only a few Black American mycologists.

James Henry Meriwether Henderson (1917–2009). Henderson graduated from Paul Laurence Dunbar High School in Washington, DC, the first public high school for Black students, where his mentor Charles S. Parker once taught. He earned his degree in biology from Howard University and earned advanced degrees in plant physiology from the University of Wisconsin, and did postdoctoral studies from the California Institute of Technology. During World War II, Henderson worked as a chemist and tested toxic gases for warfare. He served as the director of the George Washington Carver Research Foundation at Tuskegee University. Widely known for his research, he published numerous scientific papers.

Roland Maurice Jefferson (1923–2020). Jefferson also received a degree in botany from Howard University, where both Marie Clark Taylor and Charles S. Parker had taught. He was the first Black botanist to work for the United States National Arboretum. He bred, collected, and preserved cherry trees and earned international attention as an expert on flowering cherry trees. Fearing that Washington, DC, would lose the famous cherry trees, given to the city by the mayor of Tokyo, Jefferson used grafting to grow new cherry trees. He also wrote the first book telling the history of the Washington cherry trees.

Marie Clark Taylor (1911–1990). Taylor graduated from Paul Laurence Dunbar High School. She earned degrees in botany from Howard University, where she took classes from Charles S. Parker. She then went on to receive a doctorate in botany from Fordham University—one of the first Black women to earn an advanced degree in botany. Later, she served as the head of Howard University's Botany Department from 1947–1976, starting in the position after the retirement of Charles S. Parker. She grew into a celebrated teacher who pioneered new methods to teach botany students through hands-on experiments.

Tanisha Marie Williams (1985–) is a plant ecologist and botanist who grew up in Washington, DC, the same city where Charles S. Parker collected plants and made his home. Dr. Williams teaches botany at Bucknell University, where she studies how climate change affects the growth of plants. Like Charles S. Parker, Williams wants everyone to love plants. She founded Black Botanists Week to bring together and recognize Black people interested in learning and sharing information about plants. On the first day of the online project, 40,000 users visited the website. After one week, Williams and the website's committee had reached over one million people around the world.

SELECTED BIBLIOGRAPHY

Asterisks (*) in the following list indicate
the sources of quotations.

Letters

*Parker, Charles S. Charles S. Parker to Dr. R. R. Moton, Feb. 12, 1920. Box 68. George Washington Carver Papers, Tuskegee University Archives.

Parker, Charles S. Charles S. Parker to Dr. St. John, Aug. 10, 1921; Aug. 31, 1921; Aug. 19, 1922; May 22, 1923; *Aug. 23, 1923; Aug. 10, 1926; Mar. 12, 1927. Cage 319, Boxes 1–2. Harold St. John Papers. Manuscripts, Archives, and Special Collections, Washington State University Libraries.

Books

Bailey, L. H. *RUS: A Register of the Rural Leadership in the United States and Canada*. Ithaca, NY: n.p., 1920.

Franklin, Joseph. *All through the Night: The History of Spokane Black Americans, 1860–1940*. Fairfield, WA: YE Galleon Press, 1989.

Hayes, Ralph, and Joseph Franklin. *Northwest Black Pioneers: A Centennial Tribute*. Seattle: Bon Marché, 1994.

*Parker, Charles S. *A Taxonomic Study of the Genus* Hypholoma *in North America*. Lancaster, PA: Lancaster Press, 1933. Previously appeared in *Mycologia* 25.3 (May–June 1933): 160–212.

Scott, Emmett J. *Scott's Official History of the American Negro in the World War*. Chicago: Homewood Press, 1919.

St. John, Harold. *Flora of Southeastern Washington and of Adjacent Idaho*. Pullman, WA: Students Book Corp., 1937.

Warren, Wini. *Black Women Scientists in the United States, Race, Gender, and Science*. Bloomington: Indiana University Press, 1999. 260–262.

Williamson, Jerrelene. *African Americans in Spokane*. Charleston, SC: Arcadia Pub, 2010.

Unpublished Manuscripts

Burke, Janelle, and Monique Harvey. "The Life and Legacy of Dr. Charles S. Parker." Paper presented at Botany 2017 [conference], Fort Worth, TX, 2017.

Parker, C. S. "Fungus Flora of the District of Columbia and the Vicinity, Boletaceae, Polyporaceae, Clavariaceae, Hydnaceae, and Miscellaneous Groups." Boxes 10–11. U.S. National Fungus Collections, Topical Files. National Agricultural Library, Special Collections. U.S. Department of Agriculture.

Parker, C. S. "Keys to Families, Genera, and Species of Fungi." Box 11. U.S. National Fungus Collections, Topical Files. National Agricultural Library, Special Collections. U.S. Department of Agriculture.

Interviews

*H.R. 10604. "Amend to Act to Incorporate Howard University: Hearing before the Committee on Education, House of Representatives." 68th Cong. Second Session (1925) (testimony of Dr. J. Stanley Durkee).

Sinesky, Alice. "Interview with Dr. Harold St. John." Dec. 6, 1985. Watumull Foundation, Oral History Project, University of Hawai'i at Manoa, 1987: 28.

Journals and Magazines

Allen, Maya, and Laura P. Lagomarsino. "Tanisha M. Williams—Recipient of the 2021 Peter Raven Award." *Systematic Botany* 47, no. 1 (Mar. 2022): 4–5.

Branson, Herman. "The Negro and Scientific Research." *Negro History Bulletin* 15, no. 7 (Apr. 1952): 131.

Camporeale, Logan. "Heroes and Scoundrels." *Nostalgia Magazine*, Apr. 15, 2021. nostalgiamagazine.net/2021/04/15/heroes-scoundrels-2.

Downing, Lewis K. "Contributions of Negro Scientists." *The Crisis* (June 1939): 167.

Henderson, James H. M. "Fifty Years as a Plant Physiologist." *Annual Review of Plant Physiology and Plant Molecular Biology* 52, no. 1 (June 2001): 1–28.

Hertel, Karen F. "Idaho Ghost Towns: Patents as a Key to the Past." *Journal of the PTDLA* 3.1 (June 2003): 1–22.

Official Gazette of the United States Patent Office 45 (Oct. 16, 1888): 288.

Parker, Charles S. "Coryneum Blight of Stone Fruits." *Howard Review* 2.1 (Jan. 1925): 3–40.

St. John, Harold and Charles S. Parker. "A Tetramerous Species, Section, and Subgenus of Carex." *American Journal of Botany* 12, no. 1 (Jan. 1925): 63–68.

Taylor, John W., and Margaret E. Silliker. "O'Neil Ray Collins, 1931–1989." *Mycologia* 85, no. 5 (Sept.–Oct. 1993): 868–72.

Newspapers and Newsletters

"2,000 Fungus Plants Received at H. U." *Baltimore Afro-American*, Oct. 11, 1930: 2.

"2,000 Rare Plants Collected by Howard Univ. Professor." *Norfolk* [VA] *Journal and Guide*, Oct. 11, 1930: 2.

"Botany Head of Howard University Concludes Interesting Expedition in Canada." *Inter-State Tattler*, Oct. 10, 1930: 4.

*Chapman, M. J. "News of the Alumni." *Alumnus: A Digest of the News for the Alumni*, 18.9, Dec. 1928: 3.

Charles S. Parker. Obituary. *Spokane Chronicle*, Jan. 12, 1950: 5.

"Charles S. Parker." *Seattle Republican*, June 16, 1911: 3.

"Charles Parker Follows Brother into the Service." *Spokane Chronicle*, June 11, 1917: 12.

"Charles Parker Winner of Reserve Army Berth." *Spokane Chronicle*, June 17, 1919: 2.

Citizen. (The only available issue is 5, no. 11, Feb. 11, 1911.)

"Colored Men Vote as a Unit." *Spokane Chronicle*, Aug. 20, 1908: 1.

"For a Full Course: Ask to Have High School Curriculum Improved." *Spokesman-Review* [Spokane, WA], Oct. 5, 1897: 5.

*"Half and Half." *Cayton's Weekly* [Seattle], Apr. 6, 1918: 2.

"Howard U. Expands Botany Facilities." *Washington Post*, Jan. 12, 1930: R8.

"H. U. Professor Uses Auto as Plant Dryer." *Washington Afro-American*, Sept. 17, 1938: 1.

"Lieutenant Parker's Lecture." *Cayton's Weekly* [Seattle], June 7, 1919: 4.

"Marie C. Taylor. Howard U. Professor." Obituary. *Washington Post*. Jan. 15, 1991. B6.

"Negro Educator and Wife Visit." *Spokesman-Review* [Spokane, WA], Jul. 22, 1936: 6.

"Odds and Ends Aid Botanist in Field." *Evening Star* [Washington, DC], Sept. 16, 1938: C—3.

Parker, C. S. "Does Not Claim the Title Yet." *Spokane Chronicle*, Aug. 11, 1904: 2.

Parker, Charles S. "Letters from the Soldiers to the Folks at Home." *Spokesman-Review* [Spokane, WA], Oct. 13, 1918: 5.

Parker, Chas. S. "Washington Truly Prosperous." *Seattle Republican*, June 23. 1911: 1.

"Personal." *Seattle Republican*, Aug. 2, 1907: 8.

"Personal Paragraphs." *Seattle Republican*, June 5, 1908: 5.

"Preacher Spurns Negro: Spokane Pastor Soon Answered by Colored Editors of Local Paper." *Sunday Oregonian*, Jan. 9, 1910: 1.

"Professor Home from Dixie Swamps." *Afro-American*, Jan. 11, 1930: A3.

"Spokane Boys in Khaki Write Home Folks of Recent Experiences." *Spokesman-Review* [Spokane, WA], Nov. 18, 1917: 5.

"Spokane Citizen Is Discontinued." *Spokane Chronicle*, Nov. 9, 1912: 3.

"Spokane Negroes Buy Land Tract to Be Developed by Black Labor Only." *Spokesman-Review* [Spokane, WA], Mar. 6, 1910: Sec. 3, 1.

"Spokane Personals." *Seattle Republican*, Nov. 21, 1902: 4.

"Sub-Tropical Cactus Growing Near Capital: Plants in Full Bloom Near Defense Highway in Prince Georges." *Washington Post*, July 7, 1935: SB10.

"Will Enter the Ministry." *Spokane Chronicle*, Oct. 7, 1899: 5.

Online Sources

Black Botanists Week. A website that brings together Black people who love plants, from scientists to botanical illustrators and gardeners: blackbotanistsweek.weebly.com.

"George Washington Carver: A National Agricultural Library Digital Exhibit." National Agricultural Library, U. S. Department of Agriculture: nal.usda.gov/exhibits/ipd/carver.

Mid-Atlantic Herbaria Consortium: midatlanticherbaria.org/portal.

"Roland Maurice Jefferson Collection." Natural Agriculture Library, U. S. Department of Agriculture: nal.usda.gov/collections/special-collections/roland-maurice-jefferson-collection.

Washington State University Herbaria: herbaria.wsu.edu/web/results.aspx.

ACKNOWLEDGMENTS

A generous array of scholars helped shape this portrait of Charles S. Parker, including at the University of Illinois, Courtney Becks, librarian for African American studies; Kelli Trei, biosciences librarian; and Professor Thomas Weissinger, African American studies bibliographer; professor of plant biology John Cheeseman and professor of horticulture Robert M. Skirvin; Jamie Minnaert, collections manager, University of Illinois Herbarium; plant systematist Kenneth R. Robertson and mycologist Joseph Lee Crane, Illinois Natural History Survey; Andrew Miller, director of Herbarium/Fungarium; and Sanga Sung, government information librarian; at Howard University, Moorland-Spingarn Research Center archivists Tewodros Abebe and Sonja N. Woods; associate professor of biology Janelle Burke, director of the Howard University Herbarium, and her research assistant Monique Tixier; at Pennsylvania State Libraries, Alex Bainbridge, research services specialist, Eberly Family Special Collections; at Washington State University, archivists Cheryl Gunselman and Mark O'English; Eric H. Roalson, director of the Marion Ownbey Herbarium; at Tuskegee University, archivist Dana Chandler; at University of Tennessee, Knoxville, professor of mycology Ron H. Petersen; at the Spokane Public Library, Riva Dean; at the National Agriculture Library, Amy Morgan; at the New York Botanical Garden, public services librarian Esther Jackson; Director of the William and Lynda Steere Herbarium, Barbara M. Thiers; at the Missouri Botanical Garden Herbarium, curator James Solomon; and at the US Department of the Interior Library, George Franchois. In addition to these scholars and librarians, I depended on the careful readings of Stephen Fraser, Betsy Hearne, Molly MacRae, Deb Aronson, editor Carolyn Yoder, and Robert Dale Parker.

PICTURE CREDITS

To Audrey and Milo, and to RDP always —*JNH*

To Sarah, for showing me the beauty of plants. —*TT III*

Calkins Creek
An imprint of Astra Books for Young Readers,
a division of Astra Publishing House
astrapublishinghouse.com
Printed in China

ISBN: 978-1-6626-8019-9 (hc)
ISBN: 978-1-6626-8020-5 (eBook)
Library of Congress Control Number: 2022949699

First Edition

10 9 8 7 6 5 4 3 2 1

Design by Barbara Grzeslo
The text is set in Neutraface Demi.
The artwork is done digitally using Procreate and Photoshop.